I0756013

FINISHING LINE PRESS
www.finishinglinepress.com

The Lost Garden

poems by

Susan Sklan

Finishing Line Press
Georgetown, Kentucky

The Lost Garden

This book of poems is dedicated to my grandchildren:

Leo, Dahlia, Henry and Hannah

ISBN 979-8-89990-506-3 First Edition

ACKNOWLEDGMENTS

I am most appreciative and wish to thank especially Cheryl Ebenstein for her support and thoughtful feedback. I am grateful for the ongoing encouragement and response from Bianca Shagrin, Simon Shagrin, Carole Sklan, John Hughes, Patsea Campbell Cobb, David Campbell, Shelly Gottsegen, Nicky Solomon, and Margaret Spinak, along with the comradeship and support of the Bagel Bards. I wish to thank the poets Kinereth Gensler and Barbara Helfgott Hyett, for their earlier support and input.

Publisher: Leah Huete de Maines
Editor: Christen Kincaid
Cover Art: Bianca Shagrin
Author Photo: Leo Abelson
Cover Design: Elizabeth Maines McCleavy

Order online: www.finishinglinepress.com
also available on amazon.com

Author inquiries and mail orders:
Finishing Line Press
PO Box 1626
Georgetown, Kentucky 40324
USA

Contents

I. Leaving

II. Arrival

III. What is left?

I. Leaving

The knock at the door

At daybreak there was
a knock at the door.
Did it wake you
or were you already waiting?
How did you decide what to take
and what to leave behind?
We still have two things
that you packed that morning
—my father's prayer shawl
and its blue velvet bag
with his name embroidered
in yellow silk.
Did you bury the candelsticks
in the courtyard?
Or was there no time?
Maybe I have confused the story.
I do know that you left the rooms
with the casement windows
and walked with your bags
to the station.
How did you decide what to take
and what to leave behind?

Flight

When she finally learnt enough English,
she told the class how her family fled
away from the invasion of heavy tanks
that threatened and thundered
through the city.

We stayed with the gypsies in their caravan.
They led us at night across silent fields.
The border was lit with swinging arcs of light.
We had to run between light beams
to cross over.

I was afraid and wet my pants.
None of us children laughed.

To find the courage

There's the courage of the spider
to repair the broken web,

the courage of the crocus
to announce the end of winter,

the courage of the salmon
to fly upstream,

the courage of lovers
to declare their love,

the courage of women
to birth their babes,

the courage of my parents
to sing their sad song.

I'm collecting courage.
This should be enough.

Crossroads

As we came closer to his departure
I confessed I did not know
how I should be
in the next part of the journey.
He told me of an image
from Tagore's epic poem *Gitanjali.*
It is of a parent and child,
the parent throwing their child
up in the air
and then catching him.
It is like that, he told me.
Throw your love up in the air
and let go with joy.

* Rabindranath Tagore's *Gitanjali*

Lessons of nests

The nest confronts me
every time I leave or return home.
It is the bird's delicate sanctuary
anchored by a rose vine climbing the back porch.
Once there were three blue eggs,
a flurry of activity of birds
swooping, diving in and out,
hovering and then a flash of wings
within a neighborhood of song.

What happened to the birds?
Is the nest now abandoned?
Did the birds fly or flee,
heroes on a courageous journey?
Will they return?

Birds' art is to build a stick house
with no roof, open to the sky.
It is a holding station waiting
to receive a generation of birds
and launch their quest for amazing flight.

What is spelt out in these woven
twigs, grass, twine and feathers?
Will there be a slow unravelling,
a collapse softly blown by the wind?
What is spilled and lost?

A baby robin falls from the nest
to the ground beneath.
The mother bird flies down
and prances around her child,
squawking and waving her wings
open, up and down.
The baby bird watches,
hesitates, then mimicks
the mother's wing dance.
The mother bird repeats,
the baby bird responds.

Wings open, up and down,
it takes off in flight,
pumping the warm spring air.
Perched on a branch,
the mother bird watches.

Do birds suffer or regret that they
have uprooted and are gone
in exile from the nest?

Is the wisdom of the nest bittersweet -
to shelter just the eggs and fledgling birds
before they fly away?

Mandalay Express

I have a window seat on this train
and beside me is a family who treat me
as a guest in their living room.
They unpack a meal and I am the first
to be offered a wad of curried rice wrapped in palm leaves.

I want to believe I belonged
to this Burmese family
with a mother who rocked a baby
sleeping in a sarong
hanging as a hammock from the roof.

Shoulder to shoulder, passengers squat
on wooden benches and sacks
of bananas and onions that fill the aisles.
The train crosses flat rice fields
with an occasional pagoda.

This train is unable to fly,
bound down by a drove
of people sitting on its roof,
clinging to its sides,
standing on the window sills.

This train with no lights,
no water,
no timetable,
pants to a halt every few miles
at a platform beside some grass thatched huts.

Is that the way it was?
Did people really hang
outside the train the whole journey
that was meant to take twelve hours
but took three days?

Night arrives. The moon fills
the carriages with shards of light.
New passengers clamber in

through the windows
over the seated passengers.

The sun rises.
The moon rises.
It is very hot, even at night.
The train engine catches fire.
We wait for hours by the train tracks.

At Prome, bats flit
across the lantern lit platform.
Hawkers wait in case a train stops.
Children, at any hour, sell water
from clay pots they balance on their perfect heads.

I buy a watermelon and hand a slice
to the boy who has spent these days and nights
smiling at me as he hangs outside my window.
He takes it and passes the watermelon
up to someone sitting on the roof.

People settle back
and pass around a lit green cheroot,
brushing away the smoke and swarming flies.
The boy still smiles outside my window.
Rangoon is still a day away.

In life everything is moving

"En la vida toda es ir" Juan Antonio Corretjer

Rivers and tides flow,
a liquid sliding, a whirlpool,
a slow floating away,
taking off into another world.

Grass plains stir in the wind,
sand grains sifted by the air
build mountains, dredge valleys.
Dragonflies skimmer the earth.

Elephants, sharks, hummingbirds, crabs
all on the move
across deserts, jungle, oceans.
Penguins walk on ice.

Each year the arctic tern flies
around the world from pole to pole
to find food and raise
a new generation.

The universal cycle of air, water,
earth, birds and beasts
all migrate to find an opening,
to emerge into a new space, a better place.

To find an opening, to emerge into a new space.
Light from the polished stones of stars
falls to earth from worlds away.
The moon rises as is its habit.

II. Arrival

The Golden Book of Hints and Tips for New Immigrants

Breathe quietly.
Travel incognito.
Read the stars and
track the sun with the birds
to learn your new territory.
Bathe whenever you can.
Witness your children speak with no accent.
Salvage your history in your pocket.
Sing for freedom.
What do you need to live right now?
Know when it is best to leave.

Swans

Dutch sailors first sighted black swans in 1697 on what is now called the Swan River in Western Australia.

There were only white ones
until Dutch seamen found
black swans sunning themselves
by a river under the clear sky
of an unknown continent.
A sure sign that this earth
can hold everything
and anything is possible.

Black grace gliding
in brackish water,
thrusts a long neck
into the river bed,
raises a superior head
with a scarlet beak, preening
and posing with wings arched.

What is knowledge?
Black or white?
On land the swan joins the rabble
as a huge ungainly fowl.
Fierce, it forages for food.
Hissing, it lurches
with a vengeance
to protect its young.

The awkward runoff
to raise the weight of wings
as it lumbers forward
until the soft air holds
and the wingbeats sing.
Black and white.

The language of the refugee

Who knows
what can be understood
in a loud laugh
or a tender look?

The refugee watches how people open and shut
their mouths, how wide, how fast,
the way in which they turn to each other,
how close they stand together.

The refugee studies the use of the pause,
the raised eyebrow and the glance.
Men here do not greet each other
with an open hug and kisses on each cheek.
Instead they extend arms and grip hands.

How funny to be in this
new land
with no shared words
or worlds?

How to tell a joke and laugh as a man?
He can only laugh as he did as a boy,
wide grin, sweet crinkling of forehead.

Views from the train window

At the edge of each town
there is a squat building
dedicated for storage of STUFF
locked inside solid walls
for people who have no space
in their homes for all they own.

The train then passes by woods.
Through the trees you can glimpse
tents, rickety lean-to shelters,
scattered plastic bags stuffed
with sundry possessions -
housing for people with no homes.

The train whistle shrieks.
The sky is grey and says nothing.

The eyes of the street

Here is my father who has yet to meet the man
on the bus who gives him his first job here.
My father carries a jacket over his shoulder,
careful not to crease it in the heat.
And there is my mother, pregnant,
bringing groceries home in the dusk,
wearied of all the work that enters into her.

Darkness approaches and the rooms are charged
with the light of amber.
Inside, neighbors are setting the tables,
turning radio dials, pouring boiling water
into teapots and wiping hands on their skirts
as they go to answer the front door.

The baby flutters her arms out
as she is lifted high in the air,
so high she can see the clothes flapping
on the roof top washing line.

This street holds the burdens of being,
still blank and fresh.

Sometimes

> *"My beloved child, dearest,*
> *You must look into the future with happiness and courage"*

Dearest Grandmother,

My father took the courage
you sent him
and clipped it to his heart.
There was no festival
for his footsteps,
yet every step he took was proof,
though he travelled
to the other side of the world.
It was easier to be alone there
as he couldn't expect anything
to be familiar.
He was unable to carry
the feather pillow you made for him.
I want to assure you
that sometimes happiness found him.

Spring comes to South Huntington Avenue

In just a few blocks, the street hosts
a shelter for outcast animals,
a shelter for outcast elderly
and a shelter for little wanderers,
as orphans or outcast children were once called.
The street has taken on the job of caring.

Mostly it is a brown and grey street,
despair and silence interspersed with
the rattle of trolly cars and
the sirens of panic.
In the chill of early spring mornings
on their way to the food pantry,
the mothers struggle
to push their strollers across the cracks
of the tracks of the trolly cars,
their young children still sleeping
or wailing with each bump.

You can hear the cook through
the open window of the
Ethiopian restaurant.
He is banging pots, slashing knives
humming as he prepares
for the evening meal.
Perfume of cardamon, chili peppers,
coriander and cumin
wander in the New England air.
A scent sweet enough
to change everything.

Everyone arrives and departs,
the street always remains.
On the sidewalk, the linden trees
unfurl white blossoms
that bloom for one whole week.

The mother

By chance I came across her obituary,
a woman of 52 years,
who as a girl
had fled Liberia,
crossed over ocean and land
to seek a safe life.

I met her in a Boston hospital.
She was visiting her baby daughter,
born prematurely.
She kissed the infant's head
and the air around her.
Even the air around her baby
was precious.
The nurses greeted the young mother,
respecting her vigilance,
every day a long visit.

The state took her infant away,
as it had her four other children
from her bare apartment.
It had made its mind up.
Judged as a poor mother,
a single mother,
an immigrant mother,
a dark brown mother.
She was not good enough
to provide for this infant
with so many needs.

Her obituary lists her five children.
So somewhere along her journey
they were all reunited,
but I cannot say more.
It is thirty years since we last met.

Christina, I still have the photo
you gave me of yourself
with all your children.

It is a family visit, a tender one,
in the wilderness
of a child protective service office.
You are glowing, still vigilant.
Your smile shines
with the strange beauty of truth.

The house with no parents

Some of us fret, some of us bite
and some of us rock back and forth
hugging ourselves, to take us back
to the hour we were held.
No one wants to share anything,
not even the laps of the tired women
who care for us in turn.

The bath is square and vast.
None of us wants
to climb the cold tiled steps.

Meals are sour dreams.

As the day fades
at seven o'clock
we are put in our cots.
If we close our eyes tight
and go to sleep quickly,
we are saved.

The house

A wooden house wrapped in
city scenes through windows
cranked open.
She borrows a ladder
to reach high places,
change light bulbs herself.
The family settles in,
finally together, with a full meal.
Lulled by the song of the street,
they slumber at last on clean sheets.
The wind swirls around the house,
scattering the set table
and planting seeds in unusual places.
Cauliflowers bloom on the porch,
roses triumph on the roof.
The house is learning to ride the wind.

Job Interview

You are a magician
with grand titles.
You reveal it all
with a smooth slide of hand
lurking in the folds
of your cloak.
Colored scarves, pigeons,
fire balls and silver rings
glide to a command.
You present your heart
on a tray.
The applause is light,
titters murmur
around the room.

In the subway going home,
you remove the rubber stopper
at the nape of your neck
and shrink back.

On the way to work

Today I saw a couple dancing to work.
They were roller skating in unison,
weaving through heavy traffic that
was moving in fits and starts
down Commonwealth Avenue.
Not they, they were dancing,
reeling and gliding together,
the man behind or beside the woman
as in a courtly caper,
so graceful.
They were dressed alike,
telling us they were a couple,
not just two people who happened to meet
roller skating to work today.
They were a distinctive couple.
Both wore black shiny skin-tight pants,
she with a deep pink top and he in a green.
She had cropped blonde hair
and a lithe and elegant figure
and he had a square brown muscular body.
When they came to a red light,
they swung around
across the stalled traffic,
performing for the commuters.
Or did the cars stop in their tracks,
because of the power of art,
because they were spellbound by
the beauty of the human form in motion,
of men and women in harmony,
of love,
of the possibilities we can own,
and the traffic lights glowed red,
sensing the moment.

Suitcase

"I have the feeling that you lost your patience on the trip"
Warsaw, 1939

Yes, my father was still impatient
when I knew him.
He was uncomfortable with small miseries,
like arriving late for a movie
or coming home to a disheveled room.
He could only endure big things with composure,
like working most of his life
in the unsparing static
of a suitcase factory.

The Garment Factory

As the orders came in from the big stores
the foreman shouted as he doled out
the green dockets among us.
We had to calculate the yardage
and the cost.
To help us we had our fingers
and the math tables in the well thumbed
pages of *Ready Reckoners.*

It took two of us to heave a bolt.
One of us would hold it steady
while the other would lunge
with thick scissors into the material.
We could not erase our mistakes.
We paid for our errors
with cuts in our pay.
Every minute was accounted for
in the windowless basement.
A mixed crew of tired women,
everyone shouted in different languages
and smoked furiously in our short break.

Once I was yanked out to replace
the tea lady who worked upstairs.
I was glad to push a trolley
with tea stewing in a brown porcelain pot
and meat paste sandwiches.
I cut the crusts off
to make them look dainty.

Some girls had it different.
The fashion models were thin
and delicate and glided
through the corridors.
They took their time
draping their long legs
in the current style.
The managers always
tried to please them.
I was fifteen, I was short
and I knew my place.

Train Ride

We sway with the Sydney train as it
carries us to Seven Hills, through Redfern's
wet metal roofs, cracked windows
with plastic shades shutting it all out.
All those empty early morning streets
where winter rain washes everything gray.

> The carriage is filled, commuters
> gritting their teeth as the train
> shakes them awake.
> A man, elderly, Vietnamese I think,
> rocks with the train
> as he stands in front of a seated woman.
> She places her bag
> on the bench space beside her and hisses,
> *Don't breathe on me. Go away.*
> No one says anything.
> We are stuck in the tracks of hate
> roaming the carriage.
> I stand with fear in the uncomfortable silence
> with my two young children
> holding onto me
> while I try to hold onto our souls.
> As the hurt of hate entered me
> I freeze. I do not have a seat to offer
> the elderly gentleman.
> I fear my silence.
> The train then enters a tunnel.
> There is no light in the darkness.

I think of those who try to sleep
in rooms overlooking the train line,
their dreams of how to build
a better life snatched
between the racketing of oncoming trains.

To witness

You crack an egg into the sink
and there is a chicken inside.
Stiff wings curled up
in thick wetness,
it's eye sockets empty.
Your gaze is witness.

You are watching a comedy show
for a laugh in your living room
and a news flash interrupts
to show stacked bodies
being bulldozed into a mass grave.
The film is witness.

Or you are strolling down the street.
Everyone is out walking,
enjoying the spring light and air
and you come across a crowd
around a man with a meat knife
plunged in his chest,
the blood stain growing larger.
His eyes are open,
reflecting the terror of the foreign sky.
The poem is witness.

III. What is left

What is left?

Paper
We can sift through paper,
letters of love and anguish
escaped from the violence of war.

Fire
scorched all to ashes.
Buildings, bones, smashed to rubble.
There is no soundtrack left.

Water
A few survivors
fall in flight into silence
to wash up on a far shore.

Air
How to live our life?
This horror endures
in the air we breathe.

"One must remain a fine human being"

Dear Grandmother,
I see in your letters
the risks you took for love.

How you rose to the light,
despite the deadly pit
you were forced in
and how fragile are our bodies.

You catapulted your son
over the wall to freedom.
You grasped hope,
raised money to buy medicine
for your young daughter,
slipped her into a forbidden
ghetto school.

You hugged her close
as if possible
to save her life
in exchange for your own.

You breathed freely
with your humanity,
despite the horrific stench
and how fragile are our bodies.

To write was to resist,
your hymn of love.
And we have your letters.
I notice you do not write to my father
of your own mortal suffering.
In turn, he tried to protect us with his silence.

Second Generation

We wanted our parents to be bland,
to fade into the flocked wallpaper.
We wanted our parents
to pay less attention to us.
We wanted our mothers
not to sew our clothes and not
clutch us as we crossed the street.
We wanted our fathers
to be like other dads
and booze with men in local bars.

Instead our fathers
marked long hours
in greengrocer shops,
coming home only when
their sweat and the smell
of ripe rotting fruit
combined in a certain scent.
On the rare occasion
they closed the shop,
they would sit in the kitchen
reading the newspaper in alert silence.
Our mothers would continually
cook heavy meals and insist
we eat it all.
The fridge filled with decayed leftovers
to honor the moldy crust that
saved a life.

We children were not romantic about Europe
that had given our parents accents,
brown bread reeking of garlic,
dark passionate women and sad quiet men.

And We Rose Early To Swim

The sand, a slice of melon
curves against the glistening back
of the sea. The heat pours over
our skin as we step into waves.
The water is weeping with salt,
accepting the grief we carry.
We swim together as you
are afraid you will lose me
and we have lost so many.
Our bodies loosen, relax
into the ocean's kindness.

Later, we sit by the window
and breakfast on herring
with black tea.
We tell our stories,
their weight rising to the surface.

Years later, we are snared
by the flashed news photo
of a Syrian toddler in a red shirt.
From a sinking refugee boat,
Alan's small body
drifted weightless,
then washed up alone on a beach.
The sea weeps with us again.

Together we gather with the raging waves.
We rise up on its swell
to act for silenced voices.

A Sister's Visit

It's just that you always
hold my hand
as we cross a street
and feeling your larger
woman's hand
enfolding mine
takes me back.

At the barricade you suddenly
remove your jersey sweater.
I remove mine and
we exchange.
I leave the airport
wearing your shape,
not knowing when I'll
see you again.

Learning what to say

Redfern, Sydney, 1970

She was fourteen, an aboriginal girl
who hung out at the Settlement House.
She lived nearby with her grandmother
in a cold water flat.
On Fridays she would round up
her younger siblings
for a shower at the community pool.
Her life was not easy.
She lived all she could hold.

I was helping Cathy study for a history test.
The first men to come to Australia
were the Portuguese, read the text.
The first people to come to Australia
were the Aborigines, I said.
She blushed, but didn't repeat my words.
She wanted to do well in the test.

Another time she told me
she knew her tribal word
for *grass*.
This was just the first word
she would learn.

Chinese Take-Away

We can order another culture over the phone.
We dial and in twenty minutes
the fruits of an ancient civilization
are brown-bagged on our laminated table.
Instant delicacies
shaghaied from imperial kitchens,
the platters still sizzling.

We smack our lips with hot and sour soup,
relish the fine art of egg rolls
and moo shui beef served
with five Mandarin pancakes.
Jasmine blossoms float in tea cups.

You ordered a crispy whole fish
glazed with red sauce.
Greedy emperors and hungry sages
eat their fill.
Dragons stalk at our feet.

Chopsticks click against empty bowls.
We pluck over the pickings.

Singing the Blues

It was a bright blue, sky blue feather
that she swept up from the kitchen floor.
The woman brushed it into the metal pan
and thought nothing more of it.
The next day there was another,
the same soft blue fluff
trembling before the fanatic swipe.
The next day there were three feathers
scuttling between the stiff bristles.
Each day there were more
drifting around the linoleum,
settling in small piles
on the edges of cold order.
The woman continued to scrape the floor,
clanking the pan into the garbage,
removing the blueness
from her white domain.

She did not know
where they came from.
The feathers multiplied
and hovered above the floor.
The blue down blew
into the mugs, beakers and vessels.
The kettle boiled blue tufts,
blue hopes floated in the sink,
in her hair and skirts.
The woman shovelled the feathers
while considering her fluttering fortune
and how she should feather her nest.
Not being one for mere ornamentation
she made a grand feather bed,
baked a plate of feather cakes
and stitched two great blue wings.

"A change is gonna come"

Sam Cooke, 1964

Talking about the strength of moths,
how they undergo a metamorphosis
from the staying power
of a plodding caterpillar
into the grace of dustlike scales
on the beauty of open wings.
They fade into their surroundings,
hide in the silence of wool and cotton wads.
Yet when a light beams,
they fly to their fate,
their luminous feathery antennae
sensing their only direction.

Happy 18th birthday wishes

> *"Hopefully the time will come soon when we will be reunited my golden child. I press you to my heart."*

Dear Grandmother,

You write tender words
of love and hope to your son
to celebrate his birthday.
L'chaim, to life

while you are surrounded by casual cruelty,
people seized in the streets,
starving, stripped naked, shot.
Dead bodies piled in loaded carts.

The world is broken and brutal.
Days of carnage in Rwanda, Cambodia,
now Ukraine and Gaza, a slaughterhouse.
Dead bodies heaved into open graves.

How did you find the courage
to beam the light of love?
Your love for my father
links me to you.

Life pulsing, defiant against the odds,
generation to generation.
I hope I can do you justice.
L'chaim, to life.

Because

Because her grandmother's mother
admired Chief Sitting Bull as he was
led tethered into town wearing his courage
in a tattered calico shirt.

And her grandmother clasped her hands
and went to court to plea to the judge
to stop a brutal man
from plundering her good life.

And then her mother kicked her long legs up
and danced as a showgirl
with young Sammy Davis.
Fluffing her blonde curls, she partied with Sam
in a "whites-only" club.

Now here her route is of detours
to distant welfare offices and food pantries.
Sometimes she feels so bad,
she sits herself down in the middle of the road.
Sometimes she thinks of
screaming
and smashing a shop window.

But here, in a cramped living room on a thick
July afternoon, she holds her baby daughter
up to the window and teaches her to believe in
cat and *tree*
and *the rain at the open door.*

A close encounter

Unlike last time, you didn't ride a winged horse.
Instead you came back on your motorbike
and invited me to hop on
to explore the awesomeness of the sky.
I climbed on behind you
and hugged your back.
You pulled the throttle, the engine ramped up
and roared, a trumpet blaring
as we rocked off around the moon,
then left to a distant galaxy
light years away.

This journey with you was a welcome interruption
to an otherwise cloistered life.
We were, in essence, flying
at a quantum escalation in space,
looking for our north star.
Were the gods there?
I was amazed to simultaneously see
the whole solar system
and the microscopic details of swarming stars.
You showed me how to read dust
for news of the planets.

Before you dropped me back
to my home on earth,
you gave me the mission
to harness the energy of the stars
to create an alternative history.
Not being Perseus, you didn't marry me on the spot,
but it was a wonderful close encounter.

The other side of good-bye

These night I still sometimes find you.
You arrive through the doorway, your arms wide
open to me
and announce with a smile
that you have returned from your travels.
Are you Don Quixote after all?

I awake alone in the blue light
of early morning that wraps around me.
The silence is thrumming
and the hush of your absence is everywhere.

I tread the paths we took through woods,
over rocks that hug the sea.
Like the time we looked for Mars in the night sky.
Or when you showed me
a spiral of white stones laid out in a small field,
where you have to go backwards
in order to go forward.

On the street you grew up on

you know the biography of every building.
You know how the heavy rain leaks
down your coat collar
and that the fence palings
have been repainted
outside *The Good Day Cafe*
where the cook still slams eggs and toast
down the green counter
and shouts to the customers
to hurry up
as she doesn't have all day.
Strangers are familiar as they are
your old boss or your Dad's friend.
You know all the bus routes
and how to take short cuts
through back lanes down to the harbor.
Every rock and leaf is loaded
and dissolves into a thousand movies.
reruns playing simultaneously
in each eyeball:
like when the cat died
and we wrapped her in old sheets
and buried her in the sea just there.
And here is the bench where Peter Brown
and I practiced kissing
until we got it just right.

Two Photographs: After the Revolution

Exhibit at the Peabody Essex Museum

The Chinese merchant's house
shows lives through tumultuous times,
falling in with Emperors, then Red Guards,
inlaid pearl combs alongside bamboo rakes.
And over here, a photo of old Havana's
stately buildings, carved doors and arched balconies
to enter and watch another revolution.
What remains is humbled and reconsidered.
A former ballroom is now an apartment.

These Chinese courtyards and Cuban housing,
peeling plastered ceilings and faded shuttered interiors,
overlook rumpled beds, hanging laundry
and propped bicycles.
Life-packed intimate space
with thresholds to walk out onto the street
to greet what is to come.

My father's journey through fire and water

A journey of exits and entrances
began with the loud knock on the door,
led to a forced train ride,
a night of fear, huddled on a forest floor
before border guards
let the expelled enter.

The steamship *Warszawa*
loaded with refugees,
glided up the River Thames.
London Bridge swung open
to welcome them.

Next a catastrophic world war
blazed for years.
He survived.

Another ship took him to wide horizons
as far away as possible
to the other side of the planet.
A paradise of glittering beaches,
a glimmer of hope
under Sydney sun.

The graffiti scrawled on a Bondi Beach wall,
Go Home Reffos
never let him forget.

My father teaches my children

a card trick,
that he learned as a boy
from new friends he made
in Warsaw.

He holds out the pack
and each child
chooses a card
and then returns it
without revealing it to him.
The cards flicker as
he shuffles them
before their wide eyes.

He carefully lays them
on the table in rows and
a pattern that has something to do
with secret Russian words which mean
Knowledge is powerful.
I'm not sure.

My father studies the cards
and with a ceremonious bow,
solemnly plucks the pair of cards
my children had picked,

just as he was
plucked from the Ghetto
and slipped out through
the crack in the wall
before it all falls down.

The Extended Table

There are always people
knocking on the door,
calling across the courtyard,
in and out of the cramped kitchen,
giving an ear to their own tongue.
Celebrating a day shift,
a sofa from the cousins,
a birthday, the trip back home.
All those meals
with the Czech mechanic,
a large Lebanese family
that always brought fish,
two Roumanian brothers,
a sad Indonesian clerk.
An odd assortment of guests
all thrown together in this new world.
Expected, uninvited, welcome,
made room for and the put up with,
despite everything.
Shareholders of luck and what
little else they have.

Express mail

my sister buys me perspex jewels
sparkles for my earlobes
I send her a worn purple-satin baseball jacket
the ultimate American souvenir

my sister wears a sarong
as she melts on the sand
under the honey sun
I trudge outdoors wearing
plastic cowboy boots
and hack icicles from the window

my sister lives with a cat and a collection
of friends and milk crates
I am surrounded by cardboard cartons
and live with a moon daughter and a son
with a castle in the living room

my sister sips tea in bed
while reading dreams and film reviews
I crunch granola at the table
while churning over children's questions

my sister loops hopes and cinematic images
moving pictures for visual comment
I touch sweet hearts and seed pods
and gather sunspots and dictionaries

my sister drops me a line each night
to fish for my supper
I dispatch her scribbled messages
in bottles floating out to sea

on still nights we can hear each other
laughing from the other side of the world

Shall we dance?

I find him slumped back
in his wheelchair.
He sat forward
at that eager angle
of a lion alert to a tiger.
Do you want to walk?
I ask his 95 years.
He leans into me to whisper
I would like to dance.

He eases himself to stand.
Bones click, our eyes lock,
we grasp each other upright
for the tango.

We dance out the window of time,
serenaded by the fiddler
playing in the sky over the nursing home.
Hands clasped, cheek to cheek,
hips flaunted, love rolled
supreme.

Lessons of Flight

Your great weight is lowered
and your coffin is covered
with branches of green leaves
then earth.
No one stops me
as I pick up a shovel
alongside the men
and heave the red soil
to fill in your grave.
I wonder what you would
have thought of your daughter.

Lately I've been thinking
how you took me as a girl
to the theater to see *Peter Pan.*
The star was a woman
dressed as a boy spirit
in green tights.
When the show finished
I told you I wanted to fly.
You smiled and showed me how
—so unlike you, yet
you flapped your arms out
as great big wings and
danced along the crowded sidewalk.

Letter to my grandmother

Warsaw Ghetto, 1941

> *"My beloved child,*
> *I forget my longing and the pain I carry in my heart and am glad that you were given the possibility to save and form your life. Loving greetings and kisses from your Mama"*

Cambridge, Massachusetts, 2016

My Dear Grandmother,
This morning I walked my grandchildren to school.
Police were guarding the front entrance
as there was a threat of gun violence.
The hallways were filled today.
So many parents together with their children,
as if parents could shield their children
with their own bodies.
I thought of you.
Thank you for my father's life.

The lost garden

She carried the garden inside her
so she could take it with her across borders.
The lemon tree settled and its roots
grew down one leg.
Lemons, she thought, are always useful.
A Norfolk pine kept her standing straight.
The bamboo she kept in a pot,
so it would not take over everything.
Her mother's lavender clasped her heart
and urged it to keep beating.
Passion fruit vines grew out with her hair.
In the midst of her grief,
blue and red parrots flew out of her suitcase.

Acknowledgments:

Thank you to the editors of the following publications in which these poems first appeared, some in earlier versions.

Bagels with the Bards, vol. 17: "The Golden Book of Hints and Tips for New Immigrants"
Better than Starbucks: "The lost garden"
The Centennial Review: "Express Mail"
Constellations: "Job Interview"
Goose River Anthology: "The Other Side of Good-Bye"
Jam To-day: "Chinese Take-Away"
Journal of Progressive Human Services: "The Garment Factory"
Kalliope: "Singing the Blues"
Lilith, "Second Generation" (also in The Letters)
The Letters, Main Street Rag Press, chapbook 2023, includes the following poems:

"Happy 18th birthday wishes"
"My father's journey through fire and water"
"My father teaches my children"
"*One must remain a fine human being.*"
"Sometimes"
"Suitcase"
"The knock at the door"
"The language of the refugee"
"What is left?"

The Main Street Rag: "The eyes of the street"
Massachusetts Bards Poetry Anthology 2025: "Shall we dance?"
Midstream: "And We Rose Early To Swim" (also in *The Letters*)
The Muddy River Poetry Review: "Crossroads"
"Letter to my grandmother" (also in *The Letters)*
Pleiades: "The Extended Table"
Poetica Magazine: "*A change is gonna come*"
Ravensperch: "Views from the train window"
Sandscript: "On the Way to Work"
Sing Heavenly Muse! "A Sister's Visit"
Soul-Lit: "Because", "A close encounter"
Stuff Magazine: "On the street you grew up on"

Susan Sklan is a social worker and published poet, an Australian now living in the Boston area. She has taught immigrants to speak English. Her poems have appeared in *Constellations, Folio, Gulf Stream, Kalliope, Lilith, Midstream, Nixes Mate, Pleiades, Poetica Magazine, Sojourner, Soul-Lit, The Centennial Review, The Muddy River Poetry Review*, other journals and anthologies. "On passing an old lover's address" was chosen by the Cambridge MA, Sidewalk Poetry Program, 2018, and installed on a city sidewalk. Her poetry chapbook *The Letters*, was published by Main Street Rag, 2023.

www.ingramcontent.com/pod-product-compliance
Lightning Source LLC
LaVergne TN
LVHW090537110826
845146LV00003B/1138

* 9 7 9 8 8 9 9 9 0 5 0 6 3 *